T0129846

Just **S**taying **P**ositive

SERMON OUTLINES

DR. WILLIE EUGENE MARSHALL

authorHOUSE®

AuthorHouse™
1663 Liberty Drive
Bloomington, IN 47403
www.authorhouse.com
Phone: 1 (800) 839-8640

Published by AuthorHouse   02/12/2019

ISBN: 978-1-5462-7467-4 (sc)
ISBN: 978-1-7283-0038-2 (e)

Print information available on the last page.

Scripture taken from The Holy Bible, King James Version. Public Domain

Scriptures marked as "(CEV)" are taken from the Contemporary English Version Copyright © 1995 by American Bible Society. Used by permission.

CONTENTS

PREFACE

Just Staying Positive Outlines is intentionally designed to assist clergy all around the world with their sermon preparation. I truly pray these messages will encourage men and women laboring in the kingdom of God to be blessed and to be a blessing to others.

Dr. Willie Eugene Marshall

Just Staying Positive Ministries

"Clergy Encouraging Clergy"
Nationwide every Thursday Conference Call
Call in Information: 641-715-0700
Access Code: 683707#

PROCLAMATION 1

If You Can Take It
You Can Make It

"Though he slay me, yet will I trust in him: but
I will maintain mine own ways before him"

(Job 13:15).

Remember:

I.   None of us are exempt from problems
II. Develop needed patience
III. Wait on God's restoration

The Centering Moment

What is this word saying to you?

_____

_____

_____

_____

_____

_____

_____

_____

_____

_____

_____

_____

_____

_____

PROCLAMATION 2

Optimistic Expectations

"For I know the thoughts that I think toward you, saith the LORD, thoughts of peace, and not of evil, to give you an expected end"

(Jeremiah 29:11).

Just know for sure:

I.   Know you are extremely valuable
II. God is working things out in your favor
III. IGod has plan for your life

The Centering Moment

What is this word saying to you?

_____

_____

_____

_____

_____

_____

_____

_____

_____

_____

_____

_____

_____

_____

_____

PROCLAMATION 3

Everything Is Going To Be Alright

"I can do all things through Christ Jesus which strengthened me (Philippians 4:13)."

Because:

I. All things are possible with God
II. God will give us needed strength
III. We will have the victory regardless of the forecast

The Centering Moment

What is this word saying to you?

_____

_____

_____

_____

_____

_____

_____

_____

_____

_____

_____

_____

_____

_____

_____

PROCLAMATION 4

It Is Already Done

"For with God nothing shall be impossible
(Luke 1:37)."

When we know:

I.   What God has done in our own lives
II. What God has done in the lives of others
III. God can still open doors in our lives

The Centering Moment

What is this word saying to you?

_____

_____

_____

_____

_____

_____

_____

_____

_____

_____

_____

_____

_____

_____

PROCLAMATION 5

When Leadership
Needs Counseling

"Without consultation, plans are frustrated,
but with many counselors they succeed
(Proverbs 15:22)."

We will be determined to:

I.   Come out of denial
II. Realize we are human beings
III. Find the right mentor
IV. Not be afraid or ashamed to get the
     proper help

The Centering Moment

What is this word saying to you?

_____

_____

_____

_____

_____

_____

_____

_____

_____

_____

_____

_____

_____

_____

PROCLAMATION 6

Overcoming Spiritual
Post Traumatic Stress

"Casting all your care upon
him; for he careth for you

(1 Peter 5:7)."

We will not be ashamed to:

I.   Let God know about our conditions
II. Be convinced God really cares
III. Know God has the best treatment
     program

The Centering Moment

What is this word saying to you?

_____

_____

_____

_____

_____

_____

_____

_____

_____

_____

_____

_____

_____

_____

_____

PROCLAMATION 7

A Positive Family Matters

"Bear ye one another's burdens,
and so fulfil the law of Christ
(Galatians 6:2)."

When we know family matters:

I. Gives us assurance we are all in this
    together
II. Creates positivity
III. Makes love unconditional

The Centering Moment

What is this word saying to you?

_____

_____

_____

_____

_____

_____

_____

_____

_____

_____

_____

_____

_____

_____

PROCLAMATION 8

Keeping A Positive Attitude

"Let this mind be in you, which
was also in Christ Jesus

(Philippians 2:5)."

I.   Gives us a Christ-like mind
II. Produces a positive atmosphere
III. Helps us to better manage stress

The Centering Moment

What is this word saying to you?

_____

_____

_____

_____

_____

_____

_____

_____

_____

_____

_____

_____

_____

_____

_____

_____

NOTES

PREFACE

PROCLAMATION 1
A. Job 13:15 (KJV)

PROCLAMATION 2
Jeremiah 29:11 (KJV)

PROCLAMATION 3
Philippians 4:13 (KJV)

PROCLAMATION 4
Luke 1:37 (KJV)

PROCLAMATION 5
Proverbs 15:22 (KJV)

PROCLAMATION 6
1 Peter 5:7 (KJV)

PROCLAMATION 7
Galatians 6:2 (CEV)

PROCLAMATION 8
Philippians 2:5 (KJV)

ABOUT THE AUTHOR

Dr. Willie Eugene Marshall is a senior pastor, transformative speaker, workshop facilitator, faculty doctoral mentor, published author, encourager, founder and owner of Just Staying Positive Ministries Inc.

Mailing Information:
Post Office Box 10227
Dothan, AL 36304
Email: Juststayingpositive2@gmail.com

Parks Chapel African Methodist Episcopal Church
1053 East Selma Street
Dothan, AL 36303
Office: 334-794-4811

Printed in the United States
By Bookmasters